KALPANA CHAWLA

A COMPLETE BIOGRAPHY

ABHISHEK KUMAR

PRABHAT
PRAKASHAN

Published by

PRABHAT PRAKASHAN PVT. LTD.
4/19 Asaf Ali Road,
New Delhi-110 002 (INDIA)
e-mail: prabhatbooks@gmail.com

ISBN 978-93-5521-480-5
KALPANA CHAWLA: A COMPLETE BIOGRAPHY
by Abhishek Kumar

Edition
2026

Price
₹ 300 (Rupees Three Hundred Only)

Printed at
R-Tech Offset Printers, Delhi

Author's Note

The story begins in Pakistan, from where Kalpana's father came to India during the partition. His father, previously settled in Karnal, tried his luck in different cities. Kalpana, since her school days, exhibited curiosity and an eye for detail. She never topped her class but was always among the top three students. From completing her B.Sc. in Engineering to moving to the United States for further studies, Kalpana overcame several odds and hurdles to realise her dream.

The book is an attempt to bring the readers closer to their forgotten hero. The reader becomes a part of her journey and can relive the moments which defined the course of her life in the coming pages of the book.

Writing this book for me as an author was both challenging and exciting at the same time. Challenging because to find the little details of her journey was not an easy job. I had to go through journals after journals, old NASA files, interviews, reportage, etc. and exciting because I was giving life to my childhood hero in my words. It was a real learning experience for me. Although, at times, I wished I could meet her in person, discovering about her dauntless journey made me even a bigger fan of her.

The research was the most daunting, tiring, and sometimes even annoying task I faced while writing this book. Surprisingly, there is not much written about her. Going through old archives was, at first, exciting, but later it got tiring.

I hope this book brings the readers closer to Kalpana and may Kalpana lives forever in our memories.

– Abhishek Kumar

Contents

Columbia is Lost

It was 7 o'clock in the morning. The calendar read February 1, 2003. It was a fine day. The sky was clear and the sun shone bright, a perfect day for the homecoming of a hero. The families of the seven astronauts of Columbia Space Mission were whiling away their time at Kennedy Space Centre. They were waiting for the landing of the space shuttle Columbia. Whereas, at the same time, about 14,000 kilometres away, in the small town of Karnal, India, the night had already set in.

STS 107, popularly called the Columbia Space Mission was 113th flight of NASA's super successful

Space Shuttle Program. This was Columbia's 28th space mission and second for India's first woman astronaut, Kalpana Chawla. In the crew with her, there were six other astronauts, five Americans and one of Israeli descent. The mission was launched from Kennedy Space Centre in Florida on 16 January 2003. After having spent 15 days, 22 hours, 20 minutes and 32 seconds in orbit, the crew was on its way back to Earth. During this period, they orbited the Earth at the supersonic speed of 26,000 km/hr. They successfully conducted a number of scientific experiments at an altitude of 360 kilometres. The mission was going well and now it was time to return to Earth.

At 8:15 a.m. and an altitude of 140 kilometres, the space shuttle was rotated towards the Earth. The system's engines were prepared for firing. Kalpana, fondly called K.C. by her crew members, began preparing for the landing. The onboard computers and the hydraulics system of the space shuttle were configured. The payload bay doors were closed as the mission control from NASA gave Commander Rick D. Husband a 'go'. Starting with Commander

Husband, a US air force colonel, and pilot William C. McCool, a US navy commander, the crew members started donning their orange suits and strapped into their seats. The engines were fired. The burn lasted 3–4 minutes and slowed the shuttle enough to begin its descent into the Earth's atmosphere. The crew was officially on its way home.

Thirty minutes later, at 8:44 a.m., Columbia lanced through the sky above the Pacific Ocean. It entered the Earth's atmosphere at the hyperbolic speed of about 17,500 mph. The aerodynamic heating caused by the descent increased the temperature to more than 1,700 degrees Celsius. This ionised the atmospheric particles around the spacecraft, which, in turn, led to the loss of radio contact between the crew and the mission control. Minutes later, at 8:58 a.m., Commander Rick D. Husband made his last shot at re-establishing a connection with the control room but was abruptly cut off.

It was 9 o'clock in the morning. Columbia was minutes away from its destination-runaway near Cape Canaveral of the Kennedy Space Centre. Thousands of miles away in the city of Karnal, hometown of mission specialist Kalpana Chawla, people were glued to their television and radio sets, waiting to see their daughter emerge out of the shuttle with flying colours.

Columbia was zooming through the sky above Texas at 12,500 mph. The residents of Texas were taken aback by the view of balls of fire emerging out of the shuttle, followed by an outburst of sound and light. Within a span of few seconds, the shuttle was consumed in a plume of white smoke. Two consecutive explosions were reported as the shuttle was torn into pieces. The debris of the explosion fell across the state of Texas and New Mexico. A wave of silence swept across the city of Karnal.

Reporters from across the world thronged the headquarters of NASA in Washington. The officials, however, were trying to refrain from answering any questions. Hours later at 2:04 p.m., President Bush addressed the media.

"The Columbia is lost", President Bush told the media. "There are no survivors".

Karnal had lost its daughter.

According to a recent report from NASA, the seven astronauts went into a state of unconsciousness within seconds of the blast. They were strapped in their seats while Columbia spun out of control. It went into a turbulent flat spin. The pilot, William C. McCool flipped switches but to no avail. The turn of events was so quick that the crew members did not find time to put on their gloves and helmets. The rapid loss of cabin pressure drastically lowered the oxygen level inside the shuttle. Their upper bodies were smashed as their skulls tattered against their helmets. Lethal trauma engulfed the crew due to the absence of upper-body support and restraint. "The break-up of the crew module and the crew's subsequent exposure to hypersonic entry conditions was not survivable by any currently existing capability", said the report by NASA.

Although the world saw the shuttle breaking up during its re-entry into the Earth's orbit, its fate had already been decided during its launch. At the time of launch, a 0.75 kg section of the insulating foam ruptured apart from the external fuel tank. This section struck the edge of the aircraft's left wing and developed a hole, which would later allow the movement of superheated gases through the wing's interior. The investigatory reports suggested that the annihilation of the crew module winded up within a short span of 24 seconds. It began at an altitude of about 42,672 kilometres and terminated at 32 kilometres. The reason behind the death of the crew was cited to be the blunt force trauma and hypoxia. 'The physical cause of the loss of Columbia and its crew was a breach in the Thermal Protection System on the leading edge of the left wing, caused by a piece of insulating foam', CAIB (Columbia Accident Investigation Board) reported. CAIB found that the faulty design of the crew module left no possibility for the crew members to survive.

The Columbia Space Shuttle Disaster was a major blow to NASA's ambitious Space Shuttle Program. Columbia redefined what a spacecraft could do. It took off like a rocket and landed like an airplane. It was reusable and NASA hoped to make space flights a routine and inexpensive through it. It was the most complex spacecraft ever designed. After the Challenger Space Shuttle disaster of 1986, which took the lives of its seven crew members, the loss of Columbia sparked a worldwide debate over the call for and rationale behind sending humans into space.

Following the events of 1 February 2003, the Space Shuttle Program was suspended until 26 July 2005. During the next two-and-a-half years, the insulation system was redesigned and a system for the detection of an impact was installed. Had the following measures been taken before, Kalpana might have been able to make the promised visit to her alma mater in Karnal.

On 19 November 1997, Kalpana became the first Indian woman and second Indian after cosmonaut Rakesh Sharma to fly in space. She was a part of a six-member crew which flew the space shuttle, Columbia, Flight STS-87. She went as the mission specialist and primary robotic arm operator. Her remarkable performance during the mission was recognised with a special award from her peers and landed her a second journey in space, which was also to be her last.

During her first flight in space, she would keep a keen eye over the Indian sub-continent. She would point out the mountains and rivers to her fellow crew members when they flew over the region. In the words of Captain Kent Rominger, the chief of astronauts' office at NASA, 'She was known for her extraordinary kindness and her striving for perfection'. Once during her rigorous training, she lightened the mood by saying, "Man, you are training to fly in space. What more do you want?" Her contribution to the world of science and humanity was rewarded both by the governments of US and India. The then Prime Minister of India, Mr. Atal Bihari Vajpayee renamed the meteorological series of satellites, MetSat as Kalpana. The Government of United States awarded her with Congressional Space Medal of Honor, the highest award given by NASA.

Kalpana's journey from a small town of Karnal to beyond the horizon will continue to inspire generations to come. She constructed her life around the principles of determination, bravery, belief, perseverance and hard work. She showed the world that what a woman empowered with education, when provided with opportunities, is capable of doing. Since her childhood, she always dreamt of becoming an astronaut and travelling to the stars.

As President Bush remembers her in his words, "She always said she wanted to reach the stars. She went there, and beyond".

❑

The Journey Begins from Karnal

A ride through the city of Karnal does not give one much opportunity to erase Kalpana from their minds. From schools to hospitals, from roads to buildings and from tea stalls to shops, the ubiquity of her name is hard to ignore.

Located 124 kilometres from the national capital, Delhi and 127 kilometres from Chandigarh, Karnal is one of the oldest cities of the sub-continent. Its roots of origination can be traced back to the ancient text of Mahabharata. The city is said to have been founded by Raja Karna, the arch rival of Arjun. It was captured by the British in 1805 and the name was changed to Karnal. Today, located in the State of Haryana, Karnal is one of the largest and fastest growing cities in the NCR (National Capital Region).

Kalpana's father, Banarasi Lal Chawla was one of those million people who migrated from Pakistan to India during the time of partition. Her father was among the few lucky ones who managed to survive the aftermath of the partition. He hailed from Multan in West Punjab region of Pakistan. During the time of his departure from Multan, communal riots broke out in the region. He managed a narrow escape from the riots. Looking for a shelter, he first settled in the city of Ludhiana, Punjab. In Ludhiana, Kalpana's father tried his hands at several different jobs, but could never manage to make enough to earn a decent living. After struggling to earn a living, he later moved to the city of Karnal, Haryana.

When he arrived at Karnal, it was still a very small town with a dearth of employment opportunities. He started selling groundnuts and dates at Karnal Railway Station. He also worked as a street hawker, selling soaps and toffees. Later, he started fabricating metal boxes and even started a textile shop. Meanwhile, he bought a two-storeyed house in the city. After years of struggle and experience, he became a self-taught engineer and technologist and started his own tyre manufacturing business in Karnal. In those times, the Indian tyre market was dominated by foreign companies but Banarsi Lal Chawla managed to give those companies a run for the money and amassed great wealth and name in the business. Today, his company, Super Tyres Private Limited exports tyres all across the world. By the time, Kalpana's father married her mother, Sanjyothi, a young spiritual girl, whose family like Banarasi Lal Chawla's, came from Multan, Pakistan, he had become a big industrialist. His rags-to-riches story served as the greatest source of inspiration to Kalpana and her siblings during their growing up years.

On 17 March 1962, when Kalpana was born in Karnal, her father, providing for a family of 16 members, was still struggling to make both ends meet. Kalpana had two elder sisters and one elder brother. When Kalpana's mother was pregnant with her, she used to experience strong kicks inside her womb, which she took as a sign of her fourth child being a boy, but Kalpana was born a girl, a girl who was about to redefine the confines of Indian women.

Called by the name 'Monto' at home, Kalpana was brought up in a traditional Indian patriarchal environment. Like any other girl in a patriarchal family, she was raised to be meek and docile, but Kalpana had other plans. Supported by her mother and her elder sister Sunita, Kalpana often broke several traditions of her family, which came in her way. She not only went to a college, which was considered a taboo for girls in those days, but also went to study in the United States, which was near to impossible for a girl to even think of.

Kalpana was raised in a highly spiritual family. The family followed a vegetarian food habit and so did Kalpana, throughout her life. She was raised in an environment where obedience and hard work were encouraged. From an early age, she started showing signs of independent intellection. "She selected her own name", says her mother. When her elder sister Sunita and her aunt took Kalpana to a local kindergarten to get her an admission, the principal asked for her name. Sunita had three names in mind - Kalpana, Jyotsana, and Sunaina. When the principal asked the little girl for her choice, she chose Kalpana, which means imagination, a word that encapsulates her entire life.

Growing up in a small city like Karnal helped Kalpana gain several invaluable life experiences. During those days, it was rare for a girl to go to school. The trend was only prevalent in wealthy families. In a class of 50 students, she was one of the five girls amidst 45 boys. Education was always encouraged in her family. Her elder sister Sunita was more interested towards sports. Although her family was economically prosperous by the time she was enrolled in a school, yet her parents were averse to the idea of sending her to a school far from the house. Hence, she was enrolled in a school called Tagore Bal Niketan which was only a kilometre away from the residence.

Tagore Bal Niketan was not among the best schools in Karnal, but its location and management made it popular among the city folks. It was started and managed by Ms. Pushpa Raheja, popularly known as 'Badi Didi' (elder sister) among the school students and staff. The students and staff of the school lived as a family. Kalpana's simplicity and her passion for studies attracted the attention of the teachers towards her. She was always among the top five scorers in her class. Apart from enjoying subjects like English, Hindi, Science, and Geography, Kalpana took a keen interest in singing and dancing. During her free time, she enjoyed cycling and often came first at sports meets.

Kalpana, since her childhood, was fascinated with stars and outer space. The pages of her sketchbooks were filled with the images of planets and constellations. During the nights, she would stare at the sky full of stars for hours, travelling the distance in her imagination. The idea of travelling to the stars had woven such a spell of enchantment over her that she, once with her few friends, covered the entire ceiling of her classroom with stars made on a blackened newspaper. Apart from stars and outer space, she also fancied about airplanes in her sketchbooks, which soon took the form of an obsession.

In the year 1967, an airstrip was established about 3 kilometres east of Karnal. It was given the name of Karnal Flying Club and was used for the purpose of general aviation, and pilot training. Kalpana was five years old when she, for the first time, saw an airplane flying over the house in Karnal. She rushed to her father and asked, “Papa, how do airplanes fly”?, to which her father replied that he did not know. Then she asked if she could look at those airplanes, to which he replied that he could try.

In those days, Kalpana’s father owned a shop in town. After years of experience, he had become a self-taught technician and used to craft iron trunks in his shop. Around 2–3 months before she expressed her desire to look at an airplane, a few men came to his shop in a Land Rover and asked him for his time. They asked him if he could fix their plane, to which he readily agreed. Although he had never seen a plane before, he said he’d do everything he could in his capacity to fix the plane. Since he was working on another project, he said he’d able to pay a visit only when the project was over. So, the men came back a couple of hours later to fetch him. On reaching the Airstrip, they showed him the plane. They told him that the door of the plane wasn't working right and each time the problem occurred, they had to call help from Safdarjung airport in Delhi, and over and over again, it cost them about 2–3 months to fix the problem. This was a great source of trouble for the pilots in training. Once he started working on the door, it took him about 2–3 hours to fix it. After seeing his work, the captain was very impressed. He then asked him for the bill to which Kalpana's father politely refused. The captain then dropped him at his shop and handed him his card.

When Kalpana expressed a desire to look at an airplane, he instantly called up the captain. The captain agreed right away to help. The next morning, Kalpana's father surprised Kalpana and Romy (her older brother) by taking them to the flying club. She could not hide her excitement and kept questioning the captain about the airplane. The captain was surprised by her inquisitiveness. He offered the three a ride on the plane. That morning, they flew all over

Karnal. After this incident, Kalpana developed an obsession for airplanes, which ultimately led her to the realisation that her future lies in aeronautical engineering.

After passing her class X examinations from Haryana Board, Kalpana had set her mind on becoming an aeronautical engineer. Unlike other families in the neighbourhood, Kalpana's family supported their daughter's pursuit of education. Like her elder sister Sunita, she was admitted to DAV College for Women, Karnal. It was the only women's college in the region. In order to secure a seat in the college, Kalpana had to forge her date of birth to 1961 in the documents. She was underage for the admission. She successfully completed her Pre-University in the year 1977. Afterwards, she realised that in order to pursue a career in engineering, she needed to join a Pre-Engineering College. For her pre-engineering studies, she attended Dayal Singh College and passed with flying colours in the year 1978. Her teachers at Dayal Singh College always encouraged her to think out of the box and to develop an in-depth knowledge of her subject.

Till her days at Dayal Singh College, Kalpana's father did not take much interest in his daughter's career choices, but once she expressed a desire to take admission at PEC (Punjab Engineering College), her father put in all efforts to dissuade her from further seeking a career in engineering, and rather choose a profession like doctor or a school teacher, but Kalpana stood firmly by her choice. Despite all his reservations about sending his daughter to Chandigarh, he had to give in before an adamant Kalpana, and her supportive mother and elder sister.

In the year 1978, Kalpana was the first girl ever in the country to enrol in the aeronautical engineering course. She was also one of the first four girls to undertake any engineering course at the Punjab Engineering College. During the interview for the admission at Punjab Engineering College, her professors tried explaining to her the dearth of career opportunities in aeronautical engineering and the futility of the subject, but Kalpana remained unmoved by the arguments. Professor K.K. Garg was one of the two professors who interviewed her.

He, recently at a memorial ceremony, recalled how Kalpana once left him dumbstruck with her vision and thoughts. It was in April 1979 when Professor Garg was conducting a viva for his class on 'Elements of Electrical Engineering'. There were 16 students in the class and Kalpana's roll number was 15. He was asking students about their career goals. Most of them wanted to work for Hindustan Aeronautics Limited (HAL) and some of them had plans of joining the civil services. When Kalpana's turn came, she said that she wanted to be an astronaut. Most of them, including Professor Garg, had no clue what she was talking about. To this reaction, Kalpana serenely smiled and said in her soft voice, "Astronauts are the people who visit the outer space and the moon, sir".

❑

Chandigarh Days

Chandigarh is one of the earliest planned cities in the post-independence India. The city is known worldwide for its planning and urban design. The city's map and design were prepared by the famous Swiss-French architect, Le Corbusier. He changed the earlier plans created by the American planner Albert Mayer, and the Polish architect Maciej Nowicki. However, the housing and government buildings in the city were mostly designed by the local architectural team, Chandigarh Capital Project Team, which was headed by Pierre Jeanneret, Jane Drew, and Maxwell Fry. Recently, an article published in BBC named Chandigarh as one of the perfect cities of the world in terms of architecture, cultural growth and modernisation. The residents of the city face an extreme climate and an uneven distribution of rainfall, but that does not stop greenery to find its way around the city. Chandigarh has the third highest forest cover in India, following only Lakshadweep and Goa. With 8.51% of city's landmass being covered by the forests, Chandigarh is one of the greenest cities of the world. During her college days at Chandigarh, Kalpana loved walking on the city's roads in the evenings, and often used to lose track of time, enjoying the evening breeze while walking.

PEC (Punjab Engineering College), today called PEC University of Technology, is located in the city of Chandigarh. The college was originally established at Lahore on 9 November 1921. After partition, it was relocated to Roorkee, India, and was renamed as East Punjab College of Engineering. In the year of 1953, the college was moved to Chandigarh and started functioning under the Government of Punjab. After the formation of Union Territory of Chandigarh in 1966, the college came under the administration of the Government of India. In 2009, the institution was renamed as PEC University of Technology. Until the year 1962, the year Kalpana was born, the college offered degrees only in three departments, Civil, Electrical and Mechanical. It was among the first institutions in the country to offer a Bachelor in Aeronautical Engineering.

While in Chandigarh, Kalpana changed several hostels as she always found the hostel environment very noisy and distracting. Later, she rented a room where she lived alone. At PEC, she devoted most of her time to studies. Once in the evening, she went to movies with her few friends. While on her way back, few senior students of her college tried to rag her, to which she paid no heed. When one of her friends said, "They are seniors", she replied, "hell with the seniors". This incident left a deep mark on her mind. She went on to learn karate in case if she finds herself in a similar situation, she will be prepared to tackle it.

Kalpana always had the courage to stand for what she believed in. She never made any compromises with her principles in life, and always followed the path of self-righteousness. Apart from being an epitome of courage, she is also remembered for her acts of compassion, and for her benevolent nature. During her days at PEC, one of her classmates was facing difficulty in meeting her college expenses. Her father was facing a financial crisis, hence was unable to afford his daughter's college fees. The girl contemplated discontinuing her studies. At this point, Kalpana came to her friend's rescue. She started paying for her friend's college fees and continued to do so for the next four years. Moreover, she kept this truth from her friend, and from the rest of the world, until her death. It was only after her death in 2003 that the family of that girl told the world about Kalpana's benevolence.

Kalpana's peculiar style of dressing raised many eyeballs in the college. She dressed differently from other North Indian girls in her college, who generally used to wear salwaar kameez, in and outside the college. While Kalpana, on the other hand, felt more comfortable wearing jeans and a t-shirt. Many in her college, taking a hint from her Western attire, thought her to be a part of women's liberation movement of the West, but Kalpana's beliefs were contrary to what her clothes suggested. She never believed in any aggressive, liberation movement, but called for structural changes. In the year 1979, she became the first female class president of her college. After taking charge as the class president, she started working against the gender biases prevalent in her class, and had a remarkable tenure as the president.

Kalpana used to cycle to her classes and was particularly fond of enjoying the wind on her face while she cycled. Apart from her textbooks, she enjoyed reading Ayn Rand, Sulman Rushdie and Oriana Fallaci. She took a keen interest in extracurricular activities during her days at PEC. She used to write for her college magazine, PECMAG, and in later years, took charge as the magazine's editor. Once at her college's Annual Colloquium, she presented a paper on Einstein's theory of relativity, dealing with time lapse in space. This paper left everyone present at the Colloquium dumbstruck. Despite having a busy schedule, she used to find time for her college's Aero and Astro club. Once as a member of the club, she organised a screening of the film 'Those Magnificent

Men in Their Flying Machine‘, when she came to know that the other members of the club hadn't seen the film. Apart from all this, she at regular intervals used to organise talks and seminars on issues relating the role of women in society, the socio-political status of women in the subcontinent, etc. Professor S.C. Verma recalls, "She was always aware of the fact that she was the only female student in her class, but she never thought of herself as less than any other male student".

In the year 1982, by the virtue of being the first and only female student of aeronautical engineering in her college, Kalpana became the first woman aeronautical engineer of her college. She passed her B.Sc. (Engineering) with flying colours and stood third in her class of 17 students. Kalpana's days at PEC, Chandigarh, were among the most prolific days of her life. She not only learned the finer nuances of aeronautical engineering but also of life while at PEC, Chandigarh.

PEC today stands as a testimony to Kalpana's devotion and her dream of flying to the stars. The library of PEC has been named after Kalpana, while the gallery of the university boasts of her photographs of her days at PEC.

"The path from dreams to reality does exist. May you have the vision to find it, the courage to get onto it, and the perseverance to follow it", were Kalpana's words for the students of PEC from the space shuttle Columbia.

❑

America is Calling

Kalpana always believed in expedience of Aeronautical engineering. She always said that only a flight engineer can overhaul an airplane, and that a flight engineer is also the doctor of the aircraft. During one of her interviews at NASA, she said, "An astronaut's job requires a technical background and a strong desire ... to go out in the blue yonder". Kalpana had both the background and the desire.

Due to her strong desire to explore the limits of the sky and her love for science, Kalpana always knew that a flight engineer is what she wants to be in her life. The profession came so natural to her that she even had her own perspective and definition about the subject. She used to closely analyse the working of an airplane. Following the footsteps of her father, who was a self-tutored tyre manufacturer, Kalpana too tutored herself about the technicalities and workings of an airplane.

In those days, civil, electrical and mechanical engineering were the most popular streams among the students and the trend continues even today as these streams offer better employment opportunities than any other stream of engineering. Therefore, the classrooms at PEC usually had a strength of about 90 students, except for the classroom of Aeronautical Engineering, which had only 30 students sitting, on a good day. Keeping this fact in mind, Kalpana's professors, during her counselling, suggested her to opt for a stream like civil or electrical, but Kalpana was determined to study aeronautical engineering. Although about a year before completing her graduation, i.e. in the year 1982, she realised that her professors were right all along. There was a real dearth of opportunities for an aeronautical engineer in India. However, the opportunities for aeronautical engineering lied in abundance in the United States of America.

During her first year at PEC, Kalpana came to Karnal on a short summer break. Once, during her stay at Karnal, she went with her family for dinner at Khushiram Chug's place. Khushiram Chug was an old family friend. A few years back, in 1977, Khushiram Chug had his first encounter with Mr. Chawla in America, when the latter went to America for business purposes. The two later developed strong professional and personal bonds. It was during this dinner in 1979 that Kalpana for the first time met Mr. Chug. It was a year later, in 1980, when Kalpana's brother Sanjay expressed a desire to go to America, the relations with Mr. Chug came to be of utmost use. He made use of his contacts at the American embassy in order to make sure that Sanjay gets his visa as earliest as possible, and even went to the extent of accompanying him on his tour across America. By this time, Kalpana had decided to do her further studies in USA, and having seen her brother going to America, she became even more convinced than ever.

In an interview to a newspaper of the University of Texas in the year 2002, Kalpana recalled, 'After completing my graduation, I felt it was not enough. My thirst for knowledge wasn't satisfied, and hence I decided to continue my studies further'.

While Kalpana was in her final year at college, she began preparing for American universities. After receiving her Bachelors of Science (B.Sc.) degree in aeronautical engineering from Punjab Engineering College, Kalpana was offered a position with the Hindustan Aeronautics Limited in Bangalore, but she turned down the offer. In the meantime, she applied for graduate aeronautical engineering programs at Georgia Institute of Technology, Rensselaer Polytechnic Institute in New York, and the University of Texas at Arlington and had received acceptance from all the three.

By this time, Kalpana's father had become quite a large-scale industrialist. He had 24 offices in the country, and, at times, used to travel between four different cities on the same day. The day Kalpana graduated from PEC, she was eagerly waiting to meet her father to tell him that she'd been accepted for graduate program at four different American universities, and to ask for his permission to go abroad. When she returned to Karnal, after completing her B.Sc., she could not find any chance to meet her father. He usually used to be on business tours across the country. And, at times, when he did come to Karnal, he'd not reach home before 10 or 11 pm, and that too all exhausted of energy. Kalpana would tell herself that she'd talk to him the next day, every time.

A month passed while she kept trying to meet and talk to him, until one night when she grew vehemently impatient, and hurried towards her father's car when he was about to leave Karnal again. She came by his window and asked him when he'd be back. He replied, "In a month". She said, "Okay, papa. We'll talk when you're back". For a month, she kept waiting. But as the month neared its end, she started getting anxious to talk to her father. It was her mother who had to face the wrath of her waiting. On 3rd of August, she decided to go to Chandigarh, and told her mother about it.

She loathed staying at home. So, she went back to PEC and asked the administration of her college for a job. They offered her the job of a lecturer at the college, to which she happily agreed.

Her father returned to Karnal on 26 August, and as soon as he reached, he asked Kalpana's mother of his daughter's whereabouts. She told him that Kalpana had gone to Chandigarh. It was 10 in the night, he'd already asked the driver to go home, and he could not find any other means to travel to Chandigarh. So, he sent someone from his office to the driver's house, and instructed him to arrive early in the morning, at 8 a.m. The following morning he left for Chandigarh. After reaching Chandigarh, he went straight to PEC's principal's office, and politely asked the principal to escort him to his daughter. The principal was sitting next to his friend, and he asked his friend, "Do you know who he is? He's Mr. Chawla. He has money, but that is all". Then he asked Mr. Chawla to sit, to which he simply refused and insisted on being taken to Kalpana.

Kalpana was teaching a class of undergraduates at that time. The principal took Mr. Chawla to her class. When the two reached there, she was teaching with her back facing their side. The principal told him that only a few minutes were left for the class to be over. So, they stood in the corridor, waiting for her.

When the two returned to the class a few minutes later, the class was already over. Kalpana, on seeing her father coming, stepped out and ran towards him. She hugged him like she hadn't in ages. She started crying, and told him, "Papa, you ruined my career. You have no time. I don't know how you even managed to come here". A shocked Mr. Chawla was left dumbstruck. He asked her what he'd done wrong, to which she replied, "Where's the time? You don't have time for me". He hugged her again. She calmed down. He asked her again, "Tell me, please, how I ruined your career"? She moved herself away from him, and ran to fetch a paper. She showed him the call letter from the University of Texas. Mr. Chawla realised his mistake.

It was 28 August, and the last date for admission to the university was 31 August. In the call letter, it was mentioned that the subject was allotted to Kalpana keeping her career in mind, as the course wasn't usually allotted to the foreigners. She wept for a while, but later, she suppressed her anger. She said, "Let it go, papa. Whatever had to happen, happened. You've ruined my career now. I'll go next year, and I won't even ask you for money". She suppressed her tears again. At this moment, her father realised that there were still three days to go for 31 August. He said, "Why would you go next year? Why not this year"? She replied, "I don't have a passport or visa. I'm not even mentally prepared". He reaffirmed her saying, "Everything else is my headache. All you need to do is to mentally prepare yourself." On hearing her father's reassuring words, she instantly realised that he meant it, and knew that he would be able to arrange it too. She replied within seconds, "Yes, papa. I'm prepared".

He went to the principal, and asked him if it was possible for him to relieve Kalpana of her duties as the lecturer at the college. The principal was happy to help. He asked only for a resignation letter. He handed a sheet of paper to Kalpana and she started writing it. The moment she was about to sign it, she asked her father, "Papa, you won't take me to Karnal, will you?" He replied, "No, I'll go to drop you to America tomorrow morning".

Mr. Chawla started making use of his connections in order to fulfil his daughter's wish. He called the Deputy Commissioner of Chandigarh Police, who was an old friend, using the phone from the principal's office. He asked him to immediately arrange a passport for Kalpana, to which he happily agreed to and asked him to come right away. The passport office was on the ground floor of the building in which the Deputy Commissioner's office was located. On reaching his office, Kalpana and her father were surprised to know that he had kept all the documents prepared, and all they needed to do was fill out the forms and sign. The form needed the signatures of Director General of Police (DGP) as well, who again was an old friend of Mr. Chawla. Mr. Chawla called DGP's office and asked the DGP for his signatures. The DGP obliged to his request. Once all the documents were ready, the father-daughter duo headed down to the passport office and submitted the documents. Upon seeing that the duo was being accompanied by the DC and the DGP, the passport office's head speeded up the process. Later, the two headed over to the DGP's home and waited for the passport to arrive.

Few hours later, someone from the passport office came and delivered the passport while the three of them were having lunch. Kalpana and her father left for Karnal. After their arrival at Karnal, Kalpana's mother on seeing her daughter coming rushed outside, exclaiming, "Kalpana's here"! Mr. Chawla took a deep sigh and told her, "She hasn't arrived; she's leaving. I'm going to drop her to America tomorrow".

Romy, her elder brother, intervened at this point, and offered to go at Mr. Chawla's place instead. So, the three of them went to Delhi – Romy, Kalpana and Mr. Chawla. Minutes before their plane was about to take off for the States, the pilot found a fault in the aircraft when he was checking everything. The plane was stalled for a few hours, and after hours of wait, the officials declared that the plane wasn't working, and all passengers were asked to get off from the plane. They had to stay at Oberoi Continental Hotel. An exasperated Kalpana asked her father, "Papa, what will you do now"? He told her "Even God can't stop your admission. Give me all your forms".

He rushed to his sales office in Delhi, and called his old friend in America, Mr. Chug. He gave him all the details and references and asked him to get the admission done as earliest as possible. Chug assured him and asked him not to worry. He reassured him saying that he'd go personally and get it done, and would inform him as soon as possible. By the time Mr. Chawla headed back to hotel Oberoi, the flight officials told him that all the passengers had been escorted back to the airport, as the fault had been rectified. When he reached the airport, he saw the airplane taking off. He returned to Karnal.

When Kalpana and Romy reached Arlington, someone had come from the university to pick them up Mr. Chug had requested the principal to arrange for something; and Kalpana said to her elder brother, "Papa's magic works here too".

She was finally in the States.

❑

Arlington Awaits Kalpana

Often called the entertainment capital of Texas, Arlington is one of the largest cities in the state of Texas. Known for its humid subtropical weather, the climate of the city is characterised by hot, humid summers and mild to cool winters. Having grown up in North India, Kalpana did not face many difficulties in adjusting to Arlington's weather, which was very similar to that of any other state in North India.

On their way to Arlington, Texas, Kalpana and Romy's first stop was Chicago, which also was their first stop in the United States. Days before they boarded the plane in New Delhi for the States, the autumn semester at the University of Texas, Arlington had commenced already. The two reached Chicago on 1 September 1982. There, they stayed overnight at Mr. Chug's house. The very next day they boarded the flight for Arlington, Texas. On reaching Arlington, Kalpana went straight to UTA (the University of Texas at Arlington) and registered for her classes. Later, she and Romy went house-hunting, and after some struggle, they found an apartment for her to share with an Indian girl. The apartment was not very far from the university. Romy's job was done.

When during her last year at PEC, Kalpana contacted the United States' High Commission in New Delhi for the names of American universities offering space engineering, she was handed a list of 10 American universities which offered a degree in the same. Out of those ten universities, she chose UTA as her destination, as it fulfilled her requirements best. Twenty years later, in the year 2002, the number of admissions of Indian students at UTA reached a whopping 1,294.

Tracing its roots back to the opening of Arlington College in September 1895, the University of Texas at Arlington (UT Arlington or UTA) is a public research university located in Arlington, Texas. In its earlier stage, it functioned as a private school for primary and secondary level students. Currently offering 81 baccalaureate, 71 masters, and 31 doctoral degrees, it is one of the fastest growing public research universities in the USA.

During her initial years at UTA, Kalpana faced a range of difficulties while adjusting to the American lifestyle. It was a complete culture shock for her to see students entering classrooms with breakfast in their hands. Moreover, she was taken aback by the sight of students putting their legs on the benches during lectures. All of this was unimaginable for her. A girl who was raised up with Indian values, where even raising a finger before a teacher is considered taboo. Taking note of her insecurities was an Iranian classmate who had completed his Bachelor's from UTA itself. He volunteered to help make her aware of the American lifestyle. The two soon became good friends, often discussing and exchanging notes after every class. Iraj Kalkhoran, her Iranian friend, recalls about her, "She impressed me with her strong academic credentials. It was clear that she would do whatever it took. There was nothing impossible for her to achieve".

Life at UTA was one hell of an experience for Kalpana. This was going to prove very important for her future endeavours in life. With weekdays spent at classroom and library, she used to do the chores only on weekends. In spite of a busy schedule, she used to find some time for cooking on weekends. She was very impressed with the teaching style of professors at UTA. The fact that instead of assigning a lab assistant for experiments in the lab, the professors used to carry out the experiments on their own caught Kalpana's attention at first. This was very different from what she had experienced in India. A tireless person herself, Kalpana liked the laborious nature of her professors. Apart from library and classrooms, one place she used to visit with an equal devotion was the laboratory in the old building of the university. There she used to carry out all her experiments until she got the desired result. This often would cost her several hours, which used to leave her exhausted and frustrated. Although her frustration never lasted for longer than few seconds. 'After an explosion of a few seconds, she used to subside for the experiments. It never lasted longer than 30–40 seconds", recalls the lab assistant at the UTA, who also was her only companion at her lab endeavours. The weekends were for grocery shopping, which she used to do alone. She would often call friends for a cup of tea during the evenings. The discussions over the tea often used to last for hours. Her favourite place to visit on holidays was the Arlington's planetarium, which was one of the biggest in the country.

Kalpana's days at Arlington and UTA were marked by sheer dedication and hard work. Her days at UTA can be summarised in three words – perseverance, hard work and imagination. This was the first time she was living this far from home, and those were the times when there was no Internet, and phone calls were very costly. She rarely got an opportunity to talk to her parents in India.

During the first semester at UTA, Kalpana used to spend a lot of her time roaming around the beautiful campus of UTA. She was slowly getting used of the new space. The weekdays used to be spent between the classes and the library. Within the days of joining UTA, she became a darling of her professors. They were all surprised with her curious and hardworking nature. She was adamant on knowing the depths of her subject, always questioning and discussing with her professors.

With her inquisitive and hardworking nature, she grabbed the attention of people around her, many of whom went on to become her lifelong friends and lent their support to her during her days at UTA. One of many such friends was a Frenchman, Jean-Pierre Harrison, who went on to become her best friend and husband for the next 20 years.

❑

Jean-Pierre Harrison

Kalpana's name has been given to a hill on Mars, a star in deep space, college, scholarships and awards. Her story is an example of the success that can be earned from hard work and persistence, and her life serves as an inspiration to Indian schoolchildren and youth who see themselves reflected in her. But one person in whom Kalpana saw her inspiration, support and love was the Frenchman, Jean-Pierre Harrison.

Today, Harrison has a son from his second wife and runs a publishing company in Los Gatos, California. "She had that inner fire, a drive that attracted me to her in the first meeting", said Jean-Pierre on his last visit to Chandigarh. When asked about carrying out Kalpana's last rites, he said, "She had willed to be cremated and her ashes to be scattered over the mountains. We have carried out her wishes". He failed to hold back his tears while enunciating the last words of the sentence.

It was at Arlington that Harrison, who was a licensed pilot at that time, met Kalpana. He met her on 2 September 1982, one day after she arrived in the States. They happened to be neighbours. Harrison lived only a few apartments away from Kalpana's.

Harrison first saw Kalpana when he walked past her apartment the day she arrived in Arlington. Covered with a blanket, she was sleeping on the floor of a very meagerly furnished apartment, facing away from the window into which he glanced as he passed by. The first thought that struck his mind on watching her sleep like this on the floor was, "This poor Indian girl cannot afford a bed", recalls Harrison. So, on the next day, he offered a collapsible bed to her roommate who answered the door. She invited him in, and a moment after he sat down, Kalpana awoke and turned to face him. Before a word could be said, he was immediately struck by the inner fire that glowed through her beautiful dark eyes. Later, when he mentioned the purpose of his visit, she laughed and politely declined his offer, saying that she had a bed but had fallen asleep on the floor, no doubt as a result of the tiring journey which started two days earlier in Chandigarh. After a brief exchange, Harrison left for his apartment.

Very soon, Harrison and Kalpana started hanging out with each other. Whenever possible, they used to go out for long walks. The two used to hang out at each other's apartments very often. She, within a few months of meeting Harrison, realised that they were meant to be together for life. Apart from sharing the same building, they shared many other interests too.

Pierre always appreciated Kalpana's adventurous nature. He himself was a big-time adventure seeker. Out of her love for flying, Kalpana often used to visit UTA's flying club. Jean-Pierre, popularly known as J.P., was a freelance flying instructor at the club. Kalpana never used to miss out any opportunity of learning more about airplanes. The two would often discuss the airplanes for hours. They came closer over those discussions.

Unlike other flyers who take on flying out of materialistic aim of gaining control over the sky or to suffice their ego, Kalpana took to flying out of sheer fascination. Being a short-heighted person, she often had to add layers to her seat in order to reach the controls of the airplane. But she never let her height become a barrier in the process of learning to fly an airplane. It was J.P. who stood shoulder to shoulder in her ordeal.

Apart from being an excellent pilot, J.P. was also a professional scuba diver. He taught Kalpana the art of paragliding. Kalpana and J.P. shared similar interests in music too. They often went hiking and scuba diving across the States. Once Kalpana received her flying license, the two could be seen frequently flying together in a light plane. They also went to several air shows in the area. Those air shows were a first of their kind for Kalpana. They used to leave her excited beyond imagination. "As time progressed", says Harrison, "Kalpana and I found many common interests". Among the many interests that Kalpana developed, scuba diving was one of them.

After dating for a year, the two decided to take their relationship to the next level. Kalpana's family, especially her father, was hostile to the idea of her marrying a non-Indian. But Kalpana was determined on getting married to the love of her life. She relentlessly kept on trying to convince her family. The first one to accede was her elder sister Sunita, and the other members followed. Finally, on 2 December 1983, Kalpana married Harrison in a simple ceremony, attended by the family and friends. After marriage, she decided to retain her name, which was already shortened to K.C. by colleagues and friends, who found it hard to pronounce. Even Harrison himself took quite a while to get her name right. Marrying Harrison, who was an American citizen, made Kalpana an official citizen of the United States of America.

Harrison proved to be a caring and supportive partner to Kalpana for the next twenty years of her life. Their marriage was one big cultural exchange for them. Harrison used to accompany her to her

Bharatanatyam classes and also learned to cook Biryani. While, on the other hand, Kalpana started learning French. They made a perfect couple and stood by each other throughout their marriage. On the day of Columbia Space Shuttle disaster, J.P. was waiting for Kalpana with his heart in his hand. Sadly, the wait never got over.

❑

Trailing the Stars

Kalpana's name in Sanskrit means 'imagination' and her life stands as the testimony to her name. When young, she imagined to be an aeronautical engineer and became one. During her college days in India, she imagined to be a space scientist and reached the United States of America, where she worked day and night to make her dream come true.

After completing the Masters of Science from the University of Texas in 1984, Kalpana decided to join the University of Colorado, Boulder. She wanted to do a PhD in Aerodynamics under the guidance of Professor Don Wilson. She even qualified for a scholarship at the University. By the end of the year 1984, Kalpana and her husband, Jean-Pierre moved to Boulder, Colorado.

Boulder is one of the most beautiful cities in the States. It is comparatively small, with firm growth and expansion limits. This has enabled the city to maintain a slow population growth. Boulder is situated at the base of the Rocky Mountains and at the height of 5,430 feet. The city is famous for being the choice destination of hippies during the counter-culture of 1960s. The city creek runs through the middle of the town, passing by the University of Colorado. Kalpana's apartment was a few minutes' walk from the Engineering Building of the university, where Kalpana spent much of her time. Kalpana preferred the route passing by the creek, which was also her favourite place in the town. Despite being the member of the local flying club, she preferred spending time by the creek. She also started giving flying lessons at the club for which she was paid pretty well.

After completing the first semester at Colorado University, she came back to India for a break. Although she was working very hard, she was not equally satisfied with her choice of subject. Once she returned to the university, she decided to change the subject of her thesis. She talked to her professors who advised her against it but she was determined to study Aerospace engineering. Changing the thesis is a tricky business in American education system. Apart from academic reasons, one can be denied because of several other political reasons too. She could have even lost the financial aid she was receiving from the university. Miraculously, she was allowed to change it. Now she started working even harder, leaving no stone unturned to justify her decision. Years later, during an interview with a TV channel, she confessed her love for Aerodynamics. "I still have few books of Aerodynamics which I read from time to time", said Kalpana.

What set Kalpana apart from other students was her ability to win the arguments? In American universities, the subject coordinators have the power to moderate the grades of the students. No student ever engaged themselves in an argument with them, but Kalpana did and won too. She had complete confidence in her knowledge of the subject and never hesitated to discuss, or even argue over the subject.

Despite being soft-spoken, she was an articulate orator. She used to stay very mindful of her environment. She was a vegetarian and took a very firm stand against the meat consumption. "She was very fond of eating fried chips. She used to eat them all the time. But when she came to know that the oil in which those chips were fried had animal fats in them, she quit eating chips, for life", recalls an old friend of Kalpana.

In the year 1986, Kalpana completed her second Masters from the University of Colorado. This was the year when Space Shuttle Challenger broke apart in the sky after 73 seconds of flight. In the space shuttle was the University alumni, Ellison Onizuka. Onizuka received his bachelor's and master's degrees from the Aerospace Engineering Sciences department in 1969. The Challenger disaster sent a shockwave throughout America's space program. A record number of trainees dropped out of NASA's space programs but Kalpana remained focussed.

Kalpana finished her PhD from the University of Colorado in the year 1988. Few months after getting her PhD from the university, she was hired by MCAT Institute, San Jose, California, as a Research Scientist to support research in the area of powered lift at NASA Ames Research Center, California.

Kalpana and Jean-Pierre moved to the San Francisco Bay Area in September 1988. The two were not very fond of living in the middle of the suburban sprawl. Hence, they bought a house in the Los Gatos Mountains, about 20 miles south of NASA Ames Research Center. At NASA Ames Research Center, she was responsible for simulation and analysis of flow physics pertaining to the operation of powered lift aircraft, the aircraft that can take off and land vertically. She modelled and numerically simulated configurations that included important components of realistic powered lift aircraft, both in hover and landing mode. In her research, she used the application Navier Stokes solvers on the supercomputer Cray YMP, a skill very few people on earth at that time could boast of. Following completion of this project, she supported research in mapping of flow solvers to parallel computers such as the Intel iPSC-860, the Intel Paragon and the TMC CM-2, and testing of these solvers by carrying out powered lift computations. She joined the project only a few days before it finished. To her surprise, she was recognised as one of the prime and active researchers in the yearly highlights video produced by her department. She was left even more annoyed on realising that her name has been written in a poster of the simulation, published and displayed at the Smithsonian National Air and Space Museum in Washington, DC.

Few months after moving to the Los Gatos Mountains, her escape from the urban sprawl, Kalpana and her husband realised that the highway leading to the university from the mountain usually remained jam-packed with vehicles and the drive took Kalpana around 3 hours. Also, the local flying club, of which Kalpana and her husband were a part, was very far away from their house. Hence, the two were forced to move in between the urban fiasco which they were trying to escape for long. They moved to Sunnyvale, only 10 minutes away from the university.

In April 1991, Kalpana officially became a US citizen.

Kalpana was a certified flight instructor who rated aircraft and gliders. She also held a commercial pilot license for single and multi-engine airplanes, hydroplanes and gliders. She was a licensed technician-class amateur radio person certified by the Federal Communication Commission. Owing to her multiple degrees in Aerospace, in 1993, she joined Overset Methods Inc., Los Altos, California, as Vice-President and Research Scientist to form a team with other researchers specialising in simulation of moving multiple body problems. She was responsible for development and implementation of efficient techniques to perform aerodynamic optimisation. She was made the head of the team that worked on finding ways to optimise designs of aircraft by simulating the complex air flows encountered around them and studied the stability of the fluids under the conditions of very low gravity. She was extensively involved in computational fluid dynamics research on vertical/ short take off and landing.

Flying was Kalpana's first love and this love reached its zenith in the company of Jean-Pierre Harrison. Although, since childhood, Kalpana had always dreamt of travelling to the stars in a space shuttle. However, this dream of hers was lost somewhere in between studies and life. Wherever she went, Chandigarh, Texas or Colorado, the walls of her rooms used to be filled with the posters of astronauts and space shuttles. Once Kalpana joined NASA, the dream of travelling to the stars started to resurface. In those days, anyone with technical expertise like Kalpana could have easily secured a job at the Silicon Valley and lived a financially more rewarding, and an easier life. But unlike others, Kalpana chose the road less travelled. When she came across the advertisement in the Aviation and Space Journal asking for applications for a job in NASA, she could not stop herself from applying. She had all the essential qualifications and experience for the job, but unfortunately, she wasn't selected. She cleared the written exam, but could not get through the oral one. It was only on her second attempt that she cleared both the oral and the written exams. In the rage of excitement, she left the message 'I am in' over the voice mail for Harrison, who was not at home at the time. Harrison could not understand the message and called her back.

Out of the 2,962 applications that year, Kalpana was one of the 23 applicants selected by NASA. In order to be selected, she had to undergo a series of interviews, medical and psychological tests. She cleared them all with flying colours. She exhibited all the qualities that NASA looks for in its candidates - intelligence, character, integrity, team spirit and public-speaking skills.

Now, Kalpana was ready to leave for Houston. However, this meant Harrison having to quit his job and move with her to Houston. Like a supporting husband, Harrison quit his job and started packing with her. Later, for the sake of Kalpana's career, the couple decided not to have any children either.

Kalpana arrived in Houston in March 1995. Harrison arrived a few days before her. It was after 10 years that the two were returning to the State of Texas. Kalpana wasn't very fond of Texas and never wanted to return. She always wanted to live in the tranquility of nature, somewhere in the countryside. Call it the circle of life or something else, Kalpana was back in Texas.

Houston is the city where NASA trains its astronauts. It is quite a global city, a centre of the world's oil industry and one of the United States' main harbours. It has a well-developed infrastructure, famous universities and an unstoppable commercial tradition. Its biggest drawback is the climate, which is hot, humid and tiredly cruel for the 6 months of the year. Houston was described by Texas' writer Molly Ivins as "Los Angeles with the climate of Calcutta". But Kalpana was so excited that she cared less for where she lived.

For much of the following year, she and her classmates travelled to and trained at various NASA and military centres around the country as the part of NASA Astronaut corps. The training lasted for 14 months. The participants of the training were called 'Astronaut Candidates' (ASCANS).

The training consisted of many parts. First, the participants were made aware of the theoretical aspects of a space flight. From navigation to astronomy, the training covered all. Then the astronauts were asked to go through a rigorous physical training. They were checked for stamina, physical endurance and survival skills. One part of the training involved trainees being dropped into the jungles, islands or on the mountains and that too with no food and water. They were supposed to get back alive. The trainees were also trained in aircraft maintenance and repair in space. For this, they were kept in space simulators, undergoing mock drills. They were checked for their ability to survive in a zero gravity environment.

Kalpana had to endure severe training, which included activities, like learning to fly a supersonic jet trainer, parachute jump training, training in ejection seat operations and a week-long survival course. She was trained in simulated microgravity operations at a large swimming pool described as a 'neutral-density tank'. But despite all the training and hard work, Kalpana could not be considered for extra vehicular activity in space because she was found to be 'too small' for space suits meant for extra vehicular activity, commonly known as 'spacewalk'. This came as a huge shock to Kalpana.

However, Kalpana was however, offered another job at NASA. She became a crew representative for the Astronaut Office EVA/Robotics and Computer Branches, where she worked with Robotic Situational Awareness Displays and tested software for the space shuttles.

A spaceflight is not a one-man/woman job but a teamwork. The astronauts on a flight are assigned different jobs and responsibilities. Usually, a team of five–six astronauts are sent for a flight. This includes – the Commander who is generally an experienced pilot and an astronaut and is also the in-charge of the complete mission; the Pilot who is also an experienced astronaut and is responsible for maneuvering the shuttle through the deep, dark space; the Mission Specialist who is generally an astronaut with technical background and with the experience of handling such machineries in the past; the Payload Specialist takes care of experiments concerned with payloads aboard the shuttle.

In the year 2000, during an interview to a magazine, when asked what it was like being a woman in her field, she replied, "I really never ever thought while pursuing my studies or doing anything else that I was a woman or a person from a small city or a different country. I pretty much had my dreams like anyone else and I followed them. And people who were around me, fortunately, always encouraged me and said, 'If that's what you want to do, carry on'."

It was on the 7 December 1996. Kalpana was at her home, relaxing in her bed. The neighbourhood was wrapped in a sheet of snow and then suddenly, her phone rang. Initially, she was reluctant to get out of the bed and walk all the way to the telephone. She took it for any other phone call, but she, nonetheless, went and picked it up. The voice on the other side was of the Mission Specialist and veteran Astronaut, David Leestma. He asked her if she would be interested in working for him. It took her no time to realise that she has been selected for NASA's next space mission. She could not feel her hands for a moment and took a while to reply. The moment she replied 'yes', she was asked to report at NASA headquarters as earliest as possible. She could not believe her ears. Her dream was finally going to be true.

Kalpana was selected for the Space Transportation System-87 or STS 87 – the 24th flight of space shuttle Columbia, named after the first American ship which circumvented the earth. The shuttle carried a six-member crew and was due to be launched in November 1997. She was assigned the crew position of Mission Specialist 1, Prime Robotic Arm Operator, and back-up Flight Engineer for the ascent. Harrison says, "Kalpana was happy to be assigned to any mission and trained professionally, ignoring annoyances and irritations". She was going to be the first woman astronaut from India and was about to make the whole country proud of her.

❑

The Space Debut

"She epitomised the indomitable spirit of Indian womanhood. Such spirits do not die. They leave behind a legacy that must and will motivate others like her to follow the example. I did not know Kalpana, but I do know that she was made up of the Right Stuff". Those were the words of India's first astronaut/cosmonaut, Rakesh Sharma.

Columbia STS-87 was scheduled to leave earth for space on 19 November 1997. Kalpana and the other crew members were training very hard for the flight. It was a six-member crew, which included Commander Kevin R. Kregal; Pilot Steven W.

Lindsey; Mission Specialists Kalpana Chawla, Winston E. Scott and Takao Doi; and Payload Specialist Leonid K. Kadenyuk. During their course of training, the crew members were subjected to the harshest of the environments on earth. From deserts to mountains, the crew trained everywhere. They also had to spend a considerable amount of time in a zero-gravity simulator. At times, the training was harsher and stricter than that of army personnel.

STS-87 had to make 252 orbits of the earth, travel 6.5 million miles in 376 hours and 34 minutes and conduct two Extra-Vehicular Activities or spacewalks. It was the fourth Microgravity Payload flight by NASA, which focused on experiments designed to study the effects of weightless environment of space on various physical processes and on observations of the Sun's outer atmospheric layers. It also had to deploy the SPARTAN 201 satellite in the outer space. SPARTAN 201 was a Solar Physics Satellite designed to perform remote-sensing of the hot outer layers of the sun's atmosphere or corona. The objectives of the observations were to investigate the mechanisms causing the heating of the solar corona and the acceleration of the solar wind which originates in the corona.

NASA's Columbia Space Shuttle Program was the biggest breakthrough in the 1980s for any space agency in the world. It simplified the process of taking humans into the depths of the outer space. Columbia's first flight took place on 12 April 1981. The program was referred to as the Space Transportation System (STS). Columbia flew 28 missions in its lifetime, spending more than 300 days in space in total. It takes pride in taking dozens of astronauts to space. What made Columbia such a success was its airplane-like structure, which gave it the ability to take off and land like an airplane. Its peculiar structure took decades of hard work and brainstorming by scientists and engineers from all over the world. Starting in the mid-20th century, engineers dreamt of a winged, reusable spacecraft that could operate on a regular schedule. In the 1968 film Space Odyssey by Stanley Kubrick, space planes ferried airline passengers to a space station. Apparently, this is from where the scientists at NASA got the idea of a reusable space carrier.

A Space Shuttle consists of more than 25 components. The crew module, which carries the crew members, is a two-level pressurised, 65.8 cubic metres working and living space for the members on-board. The flight controls on the deck can be manually operated from either left or right. In the case of an emergency, the module can be returned to earth by even a single crew member. The cockpit is full of LCD displays and controls. There are three engines in a space shuttle. These engines fire along the rocket boosters to lift the shuttle off the pad. Fuelled by massive external tanks, these engines do not operate once the shuttle has reached the orbit. To get back down to earth, the shuttle must fire its orbital maneuvering system (OMS) engines.

While Kalpana was training for STS-87, she received a message from then US Secretary of State, Madeleine Albright, asking her to tape a video message addressing to the Indian Parliament. But, Kalpana was reluctant to accede to such a demand because she wanted to avoid any clue of political inclination. However, refusing the US Secretary of State was out of her ability. After all, she was working on a State mission. She expressed her concerns to her team and, ultimately, the STS-87 crew as a whole, agreed to tape a short video for Albright's presentation, thus avoiding the possibility of any misuse of Kalpana's name.

After days of training and hard work, the day arrived. Kalpana's dream of travelling beyond the skies was about to come true. The media all over the world was tracking the developments. The talk of an Indian girl being a part of the crew was doing rounds on every Indian news channel, magazine and newspaper. The world was watching.

Kalpana's family had arrived in Houston weeks ago to see the dream of their daughter come true. They stayed at a hotel about 6 kilometres away from the Kennedy Space Centre. On 10 November 1997, the launch day, families of the STS-87 crew were hosted at the Kennedy Space Centre Launch Director's office from where they could watch the lift-off.

At the Cape Canaveral Launch Pad 39B, the time was 2:00 p.m. It was a clear day. A perfect day for the launch. The Columbia Space Shuttle was waiting to zoom past through the clear sky. The crew members had tightened their seat belts for they were about to witness the biggest moment of their lives. The control team at the Kennedy Space Center was checking the functioning of all the equipment and machinery. The engines were ready to go full throttle.

The Launch Pad 39B in past had the privilege of sending Saturn V rockets, which carried the Apollo astronauts to the moon. Today, it was going to send India's daughter, Kalpana Chawla into the orbit. The countdown began. The engines were ready to blast and at 2:46:00 p.m. EST, the engines purged the highly compressed hydrogen fuel, creating huge balls of fire. The solid rocket boosters and shuttle's main engines generated a combined 7.3 million pounds of thrust. The lift-off was successful. At the 126th second, the boosters detached and parachuted into the ocean for recovery and re-use. After 8 minutes and 30 seconds, just before the fuel in the external tanks was about to run out, commands were sent to the main engines to shut them down. Ten seconds later, the explosive bolts broke apart the connection between the tank and the orbiter. The tank started falling towards the earth, breaking up in the atmosphere before reaching the ocean. Kalpana and her crew were in the orbit now.

To prevent the shuttle from falling back into the earth's atmosphere, the small rockets were fired, which put the shuttle back into the orbit. Once in the orbit, the microgravity started having its effect on the crew. Kalpana noted that during her first day in space, she constantly felt as if she was falling forward. She also had difficulty in falling asleep in the shuttle's weightless environment. This was normal because in the lack of gravitational signals, the brain is incapable of telling whether the body is lying down or standing up, which makes sleeping difficult. During the flight, the shuttle crew completed more than 80 experiments and other assigned tasks except for the deployment of the SPARTAN 201. Kalpana was responsible for deploying SPARTAN from the payload bay with the robotic remote manipulator arm. But because of the software problems and failure of a fellow crew member to adhere to the backup procedure, the satellite was not triggered before it was positioned and later had to be reclaimed from the orbit.

In its primary task as the 'space truck', a shuttle delivers payloads into the orbit, releasing them from the cargo bay with a robotic arm, of whose Kalpana was in charge. At about 300 kilometres from the surface of the earth, circling the orbit at a speed of 17,500 mph, Kalpana and the team had to complete the task of deployment of SPARTAN 201. The task was delayed by one day to 21 November. This allowed the companion aircraft, the Solar and Heliospheric Observatory (SOHO), already on-orbit, to come back on-line with Columbia. At 21:05 GMT, Kalpana used the orbiter's robotic arm to release the SPARTAN. However, the satellite did not start its automatic orientation. Several minutes later, it failed to execute a pirouette maneuver, a rotation around its own axis, suggesting a problem with the attitude control system. The crew failed to send the correct commands to the satellite prior to its orientation. Kalpana then recaptured the satellite with the robotic arm but did not receive a firm capture signal. Then she backed the arm away from the satellite. This apparently imparted a spin of about 2 degrees per second to it. Commander Kevin R. Kregel tried to match its rotation by firing Columbia's thrusters for a second attempt but it was called off by the flight director.

On 25 November at 00:02 GMT, mission specialists Winston Scott and Takao Doi started a 7 hour and 43 minute long spacewalk to capture the satellite. After a long wait of more than 2 hours as SPARTAN gradually rotated above their heads, the two astronauts at 02:09 GMT grabbed it using their hands. They then lowered it onto its berth in the payload bay. The astronauts were facing difficulty berthing it, so Kalpana grabbed it with the robotic arm and docked it at around 03:30 GMT. With this, Takao Doi registered his name in the pages of history as the first Japanese to walk in space. The spacewalk ended at 07:45 GMT. NASA decided not to redeploy SPARTAN on this mission. On 2 December, SPARTAN was undocked by Kalpana using the robotic arm.

Apart from SPARTAN, STS-87 carried several other payloads, all of which were deployed successfully, e.g. the Collaborative Ukrainian Experiment (CUE), which was a collection of 10, plant space biology experiments. The CUE was composed of a group of experiments that were flown in the Plant Growth Facility (PGF) and in the Biological Research in

Canisters (BRIC). The objective of the experiments was to study the effects of microgravity on pollination and fertilisation of flowers.

Due to the absence of gravity, eating in space poses problems too. If you let go a piece of food, it will float off and drift around your space vehicle. Hence, to address this problem, the astronauts in space eat dehydrated food, which is kept in a powdered form in special pouches. Drinks are also dehydrated and their pouches have special nozzles to facilitate drinking. Kalpana, during the space journey, ate a variety of food, but in powdered form. As a result, when she came back to earth, she had lost several pounds and so had the other crew members.

On the fifth day of the flight, i.e. on 24 November, astronauts Winston Scott and Takao Doi started preparing for their second spacewalk of the mission. On 25 November, the two astronauts performed a six and a half hour long spacewalk to assess equipment and procedures that will be used during the building and maintenance of the International Space Station, whose first component was to be launched in the orbit in 1998. The spacewalk included an end-to-end demo of a maintenance task simulating the altering out of Orbital Replacement Units (ORUs) on the International Space Station. During the spacewalk, Kalpana, using the robotic arm, released a prototype free-flying television camera that was to be used for remote inspections of the exterior of the International Space Station. The prototype, which in appearance looked like an oversized beach ball, was released and flew freely in the forward cargo bay for about 30 minutes. The free-flyer was remotely controlled by Pilot Steve Lindsey from the Shuttle's flight deck.

Kalpana even had the privilege of speaking with the then Indian Prime Minister I.K. Gujral from the orbit. "Kalpana, we are proud of you. Each one of us", were the first words of I.K. Gujral. The then Prime Minister of India, unable to hide his excitement, showered her with praises and felicitations. But Kalpana, as usual, remained calm and composed while smiling throughout. "Thank you, sir, thank you very much", was her reply when I.K. Gujral, without stopping for minutes, sang praises in her name. "There are worlds beyond stars, and now that you have seen them, how do you feel?" when Mr. Gujral asked this question, Kalpana replied, "It's a very special feeling sir". The talk lasted for 8 minutes. When asked years later in an interview about the talk, Gujral said that talking to Kalpana while she was in space was the best moment of his career as the Prime Minister.

After spending 15 days, 16 hours and 34 minutes in the orbit, Columbia started preparing for its return journey to home. It was time for the crew to abort the shuttle. The mission control at Kennedy Space Center gave the command to come home. First, the cargo bay doors were closed. Then the thrusters were fired to turn the shuttle upside down. This directed the tail of the shuttle towards the earth. Now, the main engine slowly started losing its thrust. The loss was late enough to permit the shuttle to reach a minimal 105 nautical mile from the orbit. After firing its rocket engines to lose speed, the shuttle now started the long fall back to earth. It took about 25 minutes for the shuttle to reach the upper atmosphere. The thrusters were again fired to direct the nose towards the earth. Friction with the air quickly took the shuttle's temperature to nearly 3,000 degrees Fahrenheit. The hottest part of the shuttle, the nose cap, and the wing leading edges were protected by gray reinforced carbon–carbon (RCC) material. The rest of the shuttle was covered with ceramic-insulating materials designed to protect it from this heat. During its re-entry, the shuttle was kept at 40 degrees of altitude. During the re-entry, there comes a point when due to the hot ionized gases of the atmosphere, that surround the shuttle, the radio communication with the ground is lost for about 12 minutes. It is called ionisation blackout. Once the shuttle successfully entered the atmosphere, it started flying like an airplane. At this point, the flight computers took control of the shuttle. It started a series of S-shaped, banking turns to slow its descent speed as it began its final approach to the runway 33 at the Kennedy Space Center. The flight commander picked up the radio set from the Tactical Air Navigation System when the orbiter was about 140 miles (225 kilometres) away from the landing site and 150,000 feet (45,700 metres) high. At 25 miles (40 kilometres) out, the shuttle's landing computers gave up control to the commander. The commander flew the shuttle around an imaginary cylinder (18,000 feet or 5,500 metres in diameter) to line the orbiter up with the runway and drop the altitude. During the final approach, he steepened the angle of descent to minus 20 degrees (almost seven times steeper than the descent of a commercial airliner).

When the shuttle was 2,000 feet (610 metres) above the ground, flight commander Kevin R. Kregel pulled up the nose to slow the rate of descent. Pilot Steven Lindsey deployed the landing gear and the shuttle touched down. Kevin R. Kregel now broke the shuttle and the speed brake when the vertical tail opened up. A parachute was positioned from the back to help stop the shuttle. The parachute and the speed brake on the tail increased the drag on the shuttle. It stopped about halfway to three-quarters down the runway. The landing was successful. The date read – 5 December 1997.

After landing, the crew went through the procedures to shut down the spacecraft. This process took about 20 minutes. During this time, the shuttle underwent cooling and noxious gases, which were formed during the re-entry, blew away. Once the shuttle was shut down, Kalpana with the crew came out of the vehicle. The world welcomed her with open arms.

The moment Columbia touched down the earth, a wave of excitement swept across the city of Karnal. The city was almost closed for the day. With only hospitals left open, everyone wanted to see the daughter of the soil return safely to earth after having conquered the skies and beyond. Felicitations from all over the world poured in for Kalpana and other crew members. TV channels and newspapers ran stories of her journey to space. Everyone wanted to know more about this wonder girl from the small city of Karnal who had overnight become an epitome of success and hard work. She was the role model of youth and women all over the world.

Unfortunately, though the whole team of STS-87 wanted to visit India soon after the flight, they could not. On 11 and 13 May 1998, India conducted a series of underground nuclear tests at Pokhran, Rajasthan. The tests created a furor in the Western world against India's nuclear program. The US imposed several trade restrictions on India and the relations between the United States and India became strained. Kalpana could not visit her native country in any official capacity because, as an astronaut, she was a representative of the US Government.

❑

The Last Flight

"The path from dream to success does exist. May you have the vision to find it, the courage to get on to it, and the perseverance to follow it. Wishing you a great journey".

Kalpana's message from space for the students of PEC.

When does the human thirst for knowledge satiate? At what point does the desire to know more and more is fulfilled? How much knowledge is too much knowledge for the human race? Nobody was, is, and will be able to answer these questions. In the absence of any clear direction, we are moving in a mindless rush to know more and more, gather as much knowledge as possible. And in this mindless rush, on 1 February 2003, the world lost seven astronauts, India lost its first woman astronaut, and Karnal lost its Kalpana.

Few weeks after returning from her first journey to space, Kalpana was back in action. In January 1998, she was assigned as the crew representative for shuttle and station flight crew equipment, and, subsequently, served as the lead for Astronaut Office's Crew Systems and Habitability section. The fact that now she was not only the first Indian woman but also the first Asian woman to travel to space didn't change her attitude even a bit. She participated in all the experiments with the same enthusiasm, and most importantly, she interacted with everyone in the same humble and polite manner. She still cooked food on weekends and watered the plants in the morning. Also, she liked to adorn the empty spaces in her house with Indian handicrafts, especially puppets and dolls from Rajasthan. And she drove her same old car which carried the sticker 'Space is our future'.

Despite her earthly approach to success, the things were bound to change. She was now a celebrity. From TV channels to magazines, all lined up her house to get an interview with her. She tried to fit in as many interviews in her busy schedule as possible. Also, she was invited to universities and schools all over the United States to give lectures and talks. She was now a darling of the Indian–American community in America. She was famously referred to as 'Miss India'. Although she could not visit India, yet she stayed in touch with her family, who kept visiting her from time to time. She also kept in touch with her alumni at Tagore Bal Niketan School in Karnal. She also made special arrangements for a yearly visit of two students of the school to Space School Foundation at Houston. The students during their visit stayed as guests at her home.

The time flew away. NASA had started preparing for another visit to space. Owing to her excellent performance during the time of STS-87, Kalpana was again chosen to be a part of the crew of STS-107 as the mission specialist. Very few people choose to don the orange space suit for the second time, Kalpana was the one among the few. Accompanying her to this time were Commander Rick D. Husband, Pilot William C. Mc Cool, Flight specialists David Brown, Michael Anderson, Laurel Clark and Ilan Ramon. This seven-member crew was going to spend 16 days in orbit.

The objective, this time, was 'to understand how human body adapts to space'. As a part of European Space Agency's (ESA) advanced respiratory monitoring system, the crew had to perform seven separate experiments and to look for any changes that may occur in lungs, hearts or metabolism while in space.

Mission STS 107 was the 28th flight of the space shuttle Columbia and 113th space mission till date. The mission gave more than 70 scientists worldwide an access to the microgravity environment of space.

On the day of the departure, her family from India reached very late. All of them combined had only 45 minutes to talk to her. Due to fog in Delhi, their flight reached 36 hours late. By then, the time to meet her was over, but she'd told the authorities that her family was going to come. So, they arranged a meeting session for them. But, for that, they'd called a panel of doctors. If they were found to be fit, they could meet her. Luckily, they all could.

On 16 January 2003, at 10:39 a.m. EST, the shuttle took off. However, what escaped everybody's eyes was a foam insulation, which broke off and damaged the left wing during the take-off. To the world, it looked like a successful take-off. Within hours, the shuttle was in orbit. The crew started performing the experiments. They kept themselves busy throughout, performing a wide range of experiments. One experiment assessed the development of zeolite crystals, which can fasten the chemical reactions that are the basis for chemical processes used in refining, biomedical, and other areas. Yet another experiment used pressurised liquid xenon to mimic the behaviours of more complex fluids, such as blood flowing through capillaries. During the span of 16 days, the crew performed more than 80 experiments.

While in Space, NASA arranged for Kalpana to have a video conference with her family. Her family was sitting at Kennedy Space Center's control room.

When she joined the call, her father humorously said, "We're old people, Montu. You couldn't have sent a plane over to us? You could've done that much". She started laughing, and said, "Can I show you something?" She took out a photograph from her pocket and showed it to them. It was a picture of her parents.

Carrying out experiments, grappling with weightlessness, homesickness, eating powdered food and then losing weight, deploying payloads, etc., none of these was new for Kalpana. All was going normally. Then came the day of returning to the earth. After spending 15 days, 22 hours, 20 minutes and 32 seconds in orbit, the crew started preparing to return home. The shuttle was turned around, procedures were followed and a few moments later, the shuttle was in the earth's atmosphere.

The media all around the world was keeping a keen eye on shuttle's movements. The command crew at Kennedy Space Center was constantly giving commands to flight Commander Rick D. Husband in the shuttle. "Roger... uh...duh" were the last words of the commander before Columbia lost contact with the command centre. Seconds later came a loss of temperature and pressure data from both the inboard and outboard tyres of Columbia's landing gear in the left wall. This was a bad news. As the anxiety and frustration swept the command centre, huge balls of fire were spotted over Texas sky.

Hours later, NASA confirmed the news of Columbia's destruction and the death of all the seven astronauts on board. The world watched in shock.

This was not the first time that astronauts died during a space expedition. Columbia's predecessor, Challenger met with the same fate, but NASA and other space agencies around the world seem to have learned less from such accidents. In such a scenario, one is left often wondering how many more lives it will take for people in power to realise that the pursuit of knowledge should not be at the cost of human lives.

Within seconds, Columbia was lost, and so was Kalpana.

❑

Kalpana: An Eternal Sunshine

What makes a human 'human' is humanity. And what sustains humanity is kindness. Kalpana lived her life with a human heart, a kind which has become a rarity in today's times. Although, unlike most of us, for whom being kind is more like doing a favour to the society, for Kalpana, this was not the case. Kindness and sensitivity for the indigent were inherent in her character. A living embodiment of benignity, Kalpana left an everlasting impression on many lives during her limited number of days on earth.

During the time of STS107, there were about 80–90 experiments that had to be performed. A scientist called for Dr. Angel, who was a professor in the Colorado University. His experiment was Exposing Micro-organisms in the Stratosphere (E-MIST). This experiment was due to be tried on the 12th day of the 16-day mission. Kalpana wasn't present during this mission - she'd worked for 16 hours before this, and was resting. The fellow astronauts tried for 12 hours to make it work, but for some reason or the other, the machine wasn't working. Doctor Angel was extremely sad because after 12 hours of extensive work, it was declared that the machine didn't work. Dr. Angel was heard talking to his colleague and saying, "The failure of this experiment has caused the entire universe to be affected". At this point, Kalpana found out that the experiment planned for the day had failed, and heard Dr. Angel's remarks that trailed. So, she decided to give it a try. Dr. Angel was delighted. She comprehended the drafts he had made, and started working on them. It took 5.5 hours but the experiment finally started working, and Dr. Angel got the results he'd wanted. It was all fun and frolic between him and his colleagues. The atmosphere was ecstatic. He told his colleagues he'd come to meet her and thank her personally when she would land 4 days later. After realising that Columbia had crashed, Dr. Angel locked himself up in his room and refused to step out of the house for a month. Finally, on 28th, he came out and wrote a letter to Kalpana's father.

Often accused of being a miser, all Kalpana had in her room were books. She used to sleep on the floor and had no furniture. All that she earned by giving flying lessons was either spent on her own tuition or to help others study. During a recent interview with The Zine, Kalpana's father, Mr. Banarasi Lal Chawla recalled, "Once a man came to meet me – he'd taken an international flight to Delhi, and then a cab to Karnal. He told me, "Kalpana taught me". "Where are you from?" "South Africa" he said. I laughed, "Kalpana reached South Africa"? He said, "She had a lecture in our university. Once college got over, I tried to find her to talk to her, but I couldn't find her". Once I did, I told her, "I can't do whatever you've suggested in your lecture". She sorted my issue out in very simple words: "Now it's my problem, not your problem". She kept sending me money, helped me complete my education. I got a job, I earn well. I miss her, but she isn't here. Who do I tell? So I've come to meet you."

Once, she kept her father waiting for long, and he got annoyed. She apologised saying she had work to do. Upon being inquired by her father about what work she had, she told him she had to get her sandal repaired. He told her, "These days, people don't even get TVs repaired anymore. Is a new shoe that expensive? I haven't even seen a repair shop around. How much did you pay him?" She said, "Papa, there is one shop, about 20 miles away. I'd given him my sandal to repair, I'd go to pick it up". She said she paid him $12. When he asked her how much a new shoe or sandal cost. '$10", she said. "I don't understand your mathematics". She told him, "Nobody goes to him to get the sandals or shoes repaired, and he stays hungry. I gave him $12 today. He won't be hungry. And now I have a repaired sandal, which will last another four years. On buying a new sandal, we'd have killed another animal."

Months after the success of STS 87, NASA kept investigating the faults and mistakes, which led to an unsuccessful deployment of SPARTAN. Since Kalpana was the in-charge of deployment, it was highly anticipated that the blame will be put on her. But after months of investigation, it was decided that it was a system malfunction, which led to the failure and Kalpana was called a 'terrific astronaut' by the NASA.

❑

Remembering Kalpana

Even after her death, Kalpana's name continues to gleam through her larger-than-life deeds. She not only registered her name in the golden pages of history, but also in people's hearts. She continues to inspire and will keep inspiring the women and the youth worldwide. What started as a journey of fulfilling her dreams and aspirations became a journey, which left behind an everlasting legacy and admirers worldwide. From the town of Karnal to the orbit of earth, the journey wasn't easy. It was full of obstructions, hurdles and difficulties. But what made Kalpana a hero was her ability to stand strong in the face of all such difficulties and obstructions.

Today, her journey is a part of millions of textbooks throughout the nation.

The immortality of her name is not only at the behest of the marbles or the gilded monuments, but also through hundreds of scholarships and social welfare programs running in her name. Here are the few of them:

- In Karnal, Chawla's birthplace, at least 30,000 school children and citizens joined hands to make a 36.4-kilometre-long human chain to support the demand for a Kalpana Chawla Government Medical College in the city, which was announced by the then Health Minister of India, C.P. Thakur and later promised by Prime Minister of India, Manmohan Singh. The Kalpana Chawla Medical College Nirman Committee, the committee responsible for constructing the college, was backed by volunteers and activists of various organisations, supported by students from 34 schools. They swarmed the roads and formed a chain along the roads in Karnal to demonstrate that they continued to revere Chawla as an outstanding astronaut. On 18 November 2013, the foundation stone of the college was laid in her memory by the State Government.

- Asteroid 51826 Kalpana Chawla, one of the seven named after the Columbia's crew.
- The Kalpana Chawla ISU Scholarship fund was founded by alumni of the International Space University (ISU) in 2010 to support Indian student participation in international space education programs.
- The Kalpana Chawla Memorial Scholarship program was instituted by the Indian Students Association (ISA) at the University of Texas at El Paso (UTEP) in 2005 for the meritorious graduate students.
- On 5 February 2003, India's Prime Minister, Mr. Atal Bihari Vajpayee announced that the meteorological series of satellites, MetSat, was to be renamed as 'Kalpana'. The first satellite of the series, 'MetSat-1', launched by India on 12 September 2002, is now known as

'Kalpana-1'. 'Kalpana-2' was expected to be launched by 2007.

- 74th Street in Jackson Heights, Queens, New York City has been renamed 74th Street Kalpana Chawla Way in her honour.

- The Kalpana Chawla Outstanding Recent Alumni Award at the University of Colorado, given since 1983, was renamed for Chawla.

- The University of Texas at Arlington, where Chawla obtained a Master of Science degree in aerospace engineering in 1984, opened a dormitory named Kalpana Chawla Hall in 2004.

- The Kalpana Chawla Award was instituted by the Government of Karnataka in 2004 for the young women scientists.

- The girls' hostel at Punjab Engineering College is named after Chawla. In addition, an award of INR twenty-five thousand, a medal, and a certificate is instituted for the best student in the Aeronautical Engineering department.

- NASA has dedicated a supercomputer to Chawla.
- One of Florida Institute of Technology's students apartment complexes, Columbia Village Suites, has halls named after each of the astronauts, including Chawla.
- The NASA Mars Exploration Rover mission has named seven peaks in a chain of hills, named the Columbia Hills, after each of the seven astronauts lost in the Columbia shuttle disaster. One of them is Chawla Hill, named after Chawla.
- Steve Morse from the band Deep Purple created the song 'Contact Lost' in memory of the Columbia tragedy along with her interest in the band. The song can be found on the album Bananas.
- Novelist Peter David named a shuttlecraft the Chawla after the astronaut in his 2007 Star Trek novel Star Trek: The Next Generation: Before Dishonour.

- The University of Texas at Arlington dedicated the Kalpana Chawla Memorial on 3 May 2010, in Nedderman Hall, one of the primary buildings in the College of Engineering.

- The Government of Haryana established the Kalpana Chawla Planetarium in Jyotisar, Kurukshetra.

- The Indian Institute of Technology, Kharagpur, named the Kalpana Chawla Space Technology Cell in her honour.

- A military housing development at Naval Air Station Patuxent River, Maryland, has been named Columbia Colony and includes a street named Chawla Way.

❑